OVER THE
SANTA FE TRAIL
1857

PUNCHED HIM WITH THE POINT

OVER THE
SANTA FE TRAIL
1857

❧ From the original 1905 edition by
William B. Napton. ❧ Introduction
by Donald C. Cutter ❧ Published by
the Stagecoach Press, Santa Fe, 1964

First Regular Edition

Frontispiece from original 1905 edition.

STAGECOACH PRESS, BOX 921, SANTA FE, N. M.

Introduction

THE SANTA FE TRAIL—what visions of yesteryear are con-
jured by that single phrase! One of the best known stories
of Western America, it is first the tale of Manifest Destiny
being applied to the northern frontier of the newly born
Mexican nation, and subsequently, after 1848, the story of
the tenuous lifeline that maintained connection between the
States and the recently acquired, sparsely settled Southwest.

Since the story of the Santa Fé trade has been frequently
told, one can visualize the early tentative approach of the
American traders, followed in a few short years by "organi-
zation" of the trade on a caravan basis, with cumbersome
wagons assembling at Council Grove for passage through
Indian Country. Here and there deep furrows of century
old wagon ruts still corrugate the prairie sod, and one can
imagine the laborious, plodding steps of slow moving oxen,
the crack of the bullwhip, the occasional U.S. or Mexican
military escort, the long weeks on the trail, and finally the
traditional pellmell dash of men and merchandise laden
wagons for their final goal of the sleepy village at the base
of the Sangre de Cristos. These are the romantic elements
and well deserve to live in heroic relief.

But after the Mexican War was over and international
complications were eliminated, the Santa Fé trade enjoyed
a long, uninterrupted period of less glamorous but more ef-

fective supply of the Southwest. It is from this more pro-
saic and historically neglected period that the account of
William B. Napton comes, and though by 1857 the trade
had become in large measure routine in character, it is pre-
cisely for this reason that accounts such as his become important sources of Western American history, for by Napton's
time participants had largely ceased to view their activities
as sufficiently unique to demand contemporary journalistic
treatment. It is fortunate that the author later considered
his youthful experiences as of sufficient interest to be re-
corded in this single small volume, published in only one
edition in 1905 by the Franklin Hudson Publishing Company of Kansas City Missouri, and entitled *Over the Santa
Fé Trail, 1857.* Most of this original edition was issued with
pictorial wrappers, and was probably privately financed by
the author, as was the case with other memoirs published
at that time and place. Its publication may have encouraged
the appearance of a similar work by William Ryus published
at Kansas City in 1913 under the title of *The Second William Penn; Treating With Indians on the Santa Fé Trail,
1860-66.*

According to his own dates, Napton was born in 1839
and was subsequently raised in Saline County, Missouri.
In 1857, as an eighteen year old, he journeyed to Santa Fé
and back with a wagon train commanded by "Jim Crow"
Chiles, a son of Colonel James Chiles of nearby Jackson
County. In 1858 the youthful Napton was an attaché at
the Blackfoot Indian agency on Sun River, and the last one

fourth of his slim 1905 volume was dedicated to these experiences. This section, entitled "Lewis & Clark's Route Retraveled; the Upper Missouri in 1858," is omitted from the present reprint since it does not relate to Napton's Santa Fé Trail activity.

Napton's book is relatively unknown to Western Americana bibliographers although Wright Howes lists it as item N-9 in his *US-iana* (second edition). A copy was sold at the auction of the Holliday collection in 1954. Earlier, in 1939, one copy was offered at $20.00, and by 1955 the market price had risen to $45.00. Doubtless today's price would be appreciably higher. It is felt that the scarcity and utility of this account of one of the last paragraphs of an important chapter of American history justify its reappearance.

A photocopy of the original was made available from the Frank Phillips Collection at the University of Oklahoma Library, for which grateful acknowledgment is made. Particular appreciation is due to Dr. Arthur McAnally and to Dr. A. M. Gibson of that library for assistance. The present reprint faithfully conserves the original, including the illustrations, and adds a few footnotes to Napton's own.

—DONALD C. CUTTER

1

Captain "Jim Crow" Chiles

WHEN I was a lad of 12 years of age my father had a red-headed overseer, good-natured and fond of telling stories, the kind that suited the understanding and tickled the fancy of a boy. His stories were always related as being truthful accounts of actual occurrences, although I suspected they were frequently creatures of his own imagination. This overseer, a Westerner born and bred, had driven an ox wagon in a train across the plains to New Mexico; had made two trips across—in 1847 and 1848—one extending as far as Chihuahua, in Old Mexico. His observation was keen, and his memory unexcelled, so that, years afterwards, he could relate, in minute detail, the events of every day's travel, from the beginning to the end of the journey. I was charmed with his accounts of the Indians and buffalo, wolves, antelope and prairie dogs.

Reaching the age of 18 in 1857, with indifferent health, my father acquiesced in my determination to cross the plains to New Mexico. The doctor said the journey would benefit my health. Already an expert with a gun or pistol, I had killed all kinds of game to be found in Missouri, and had read Gordon Cumming's book of his hunting exploits in South Africa, so that I felt as if nothing less than killing big game, like buffalo and elk, could gratify my sporting proclivities.

Colonel James Chiles of "Six Mile," Jackson County, was a state senator, and while at Jefferson City during the session of the legislature, my father telling him of my desire to go out to Santa Fé, the colonel sent me an invitation to come to his house by the middle of April and go out with a train belonging to his son. So in the early spring of 1857 I set out from my home in Saline County,* well mounted and equipped for the journey.

The spring was backward, and when I reached Colonel Chile's house in the middle of April winter was still "lingering in the lap of spring." The grass was not good on the plains until the 10th of May. It was arranged for me to go out with the train commanded by "Jim Crow," a son of Colonel Chiles.

"Jim Crow" was then about twenty-five, not over medium height, but strong, athletic and wiry, and had a pretty well established reputation as a fighter among the frontiersmen. He had killed a lawyer named Moore, who lived at Leavenworth, in the Noland hotel at Independence. After the Civil War he killed two other men at Independence, and he himself was eventually killed in a fight with the Independence

*Saline County is in central Missouri, 70 miles east of Independence.

town marshal. But I found "Jim Crow" a kind and consider-
ate friend, jovial and good natured generally, but subject to
violent fits of anger, and when angry, a very dangerous man.
One night on the "trail," while he and I were riding some distance ahead of the train, amid the solitude of the darkness
and the vast plains, the conversation drifted into a confiden-
tial vein. He recalled the killing of Moore, saying he regret-
ted it beyond measure; that the affair had haunted him day
and night; that he would willingly give up all that he owned
or expected to acquire to be relieved of the anguish and trouble and remorse the act had caused him. But he was possessed of the kind of courage and combativeness which never
suggested the avoidance of a fight then or afterward.

Kansas City was even then, in 1857, an aspiring town. For
a month or two in the spring the levee was covered with
wagons and teams, and sometimes four or five steamboats
were at the wharf discharging freight. General John W. Reid
had recently bought forty acres, the northwest corner of
which is now the intersection of Broadway and Twelfth
street, for $2,000. The land was covered with timber, which
he cut into cord wood and sold to the steamboats for about
enough to pay for the land.

There were no streets, and only one road from the levee,
leaving the river front at Grand avenue, running obliquely
across to Main street and back again to Grand avenue, in
McGee's addition. Colonel Milton McGee had taken down
his fences and laid off his cornfields into lots.

The work cattle and wagons were collected and a camp

11 🕮

established, about the first of May, on the high, rolling prairie near the Santa Fé trail, three miles southwest of Westport. The wagons were heavy, cumbrous affairs with long deep beds, covered with sheets of heavy cotton cloth, supported by bows. A man six feet high could stand erect in one of them, and they were designed to hold a load of seven or eight thousand pounds of merchandise each. Those in our train were made by Hiram Young, a free negro at Independence, and they were considered as good as any except those with iron axles. The freight consisted of merchandise for the trade in New Mexico. Two of the wagons were loaded with imported champagne for Colonel St. Vrain of Las Vegas and Mora.

There was a shortage of good ox drivers that spring and Captain "Jim Crow" found it difficult to supply the number he needed. Twenty-five dollars a month "and found" were the wages. One evening, while we were lounging around the corral, waiting for supper, three men came up on foot, inquiring for the captain of the train. They were good looking, well dressed men, two of them wearing silk hats, but bearing no resemblance to the ordinary ox driver. They said they were stranded and looking for work. They proposed to Captain Chiles to hire to him for drivers, while they disclaimed any knowledge of the calling.

"Jim Crow" laughed, and after interrogating them as to their antecedents, said he would hire them on probation. "I will take you along," he said, "and if I find you can learn to drive cattle before we get to Council Grove, the last settlement on the road, then I'll keep you; otherwise not, and you must look out for yourselves."

They were invited to supper and assigned to a mess. One of them was named Whitcom. He hailed from Massachusetts and had never seen a yoke of oxen in his life, but he was strong, sturdy and active, and before we reached New Mexico he was rated the most dexterous driver in the outfit. Moreover, his team looked better than any in the train when we reached the end of our journey. Ten years ago Whitcom was living in Cheyenne, and was one of the wealthiest cattle raisers in the state of Wyoming.

Another of the three hailed from Cincinnati. He wore a threadbare suit of broadcloth and a "plug" hat, and was tall, angular, awkward, slip-shod and slouchy in appearance. He had been employed in his father's banking house in Cincinnati, and was accomplished in penmanship and a good accountant; but he proved to be utterly unfit for an ox driver. He could not hold his own among his rough companions, and became the object of their jeers and derision. By unanimous consent he was given the name of "Skeesicks," and by this name he was known ever afterwards.

The third of the trio proved to be a fairly good driver, and is now a prosperous merchant in the state of Montana.

Among the drivers was a young Mexican, Juan, who had been in the employ of the Chiles brothers for years. Through him we were enabled to converse with the Kiowas and Comanches when we reached them. Many of the Indians could speak or understand Spanish, but could not understand a word of English. We had men among the teamsters from Tennessee, Kentucky, Arkansas and Texas. They soon became known and answered to the name of their own state. "Tennessee" and "Texas" prided themselves on the size and weight of their whips, and the loudness of the noise they could make in popping them.

Young Reece, from Missouri, went out with the train for his health. He had consumption and hoped the journey over the plains would be of benefit to him. He was very tall, being six feet four inches, of large bone and frame, but thin as a huge skeleton, and had allowed his heavy black hair to grow until it hung below his shoulders. He was well off so far as property was concerned, and rode a splendid dapple gray horse, muscular, tough and graceful, with handsome mane and tail, which could fairly fly over the prairie.

2

In Camp, South of Westport

IN the camp, three miles southwest of Westport, we were detained for a fortnight or more, awaiting the arrival of our freight at Kansas City. There were twenty-six wagon, five yoke of oxen to each, carrying about seven thousand pounds of freight each. There were no tents, so we slept on the ground, either under a wagon or, if we preferred it, the broad canopy of heaven.

Captain "Jim Crow" commanded the company, with Rice as assistant wagonmaster. There was one driver for each wagon, and a boy of 16, of frontier origin and training, whose duty it was to drive the "cavayard"* or loose cattle, taken along in case any of the teams should get lame or unfit for service. "Jim Crow," immediately on his arrival at the camp, gave the boy the nickname of "Little Breeches," suggested by his very tight-fitting trousers, and the name, abbreviated to "Little Breech," stuck to him.

While encamped below Westport I was fortunate in pur-

*Caballada; a horse herd.

chasing a first rate "buffalo horse," a California "lass horse," that had been brought across the plains the previous year. He proved his excellence afterward, was very fast and would run up so close to a buffalo that I could sometimes touch him with the pistol point.

Camped in our vicinity were several corrals of trains belonging to Mexican merchants, who used mules instead of oxen, and had lately come up from New Mexico. These Mexicans subsisted altogether on taos* (unbolted) flour, and dried buffalo meat, while our mess wagon was filled with side bacon, flour, coffee, sugar, beans and pickles.

I soon got on fair terms of acquaintance with the master of one of these Spanish trains. He was a successful buffalo hunter, but I was surprised to find he used a spear for killing them, instead of a pistol. When a buffalo was found at a distance from the road or camp he would goad the animal, until so enraged, it would turn upon and follow him, and in this manner he would get the game to a more convenient place for butchering, before finally dispatching it.

There were no farms fenced up in sight of our camp at that time, but the prairie was dotted with the houses of the "squatter sovereigns," who were "holding down" claims.

On the 10th day of June we yoked up and started on the long journey. At the outset everybody about the train, from the captain to the cavayard driver, was filled with good humor. The weather was perfect, the view of the apparently

---

*A type of coarsely ground corn flour produced at Taos and widely distributed by traders.

📖 16

boundless prairie exhilarating. The road having been surveyed and established by the government before the country was at all occupied, was almost as straight as an arrow toward the southwest. The wagonmaster would arouse the men before daylight in the morning and the cattle would be driven up to the corral, yoked up and hitched to the wagons by the time the cooks could prepare breakfast, a cook being assigned to each six or eight men. Some of the oxen were not well broken to the yoke, and it was a difficult task at the dim break of day for a green man to select each steer that belonged to his team in the corral, where the 250 were crowded together so that their sides would almost touch.

Once on the road the drive was continued for from eight to twelve miles, the stops being governed by the convenience of camping-places, where grass and water could be found for the cattle. Familiarity with the route was essential in the wagonmaster, who, riding some distance ahead, would select the camping-place, and when the train came up direct the formation of the corral. The cattle were immediately unyoked and turned loose, herded by two of the teamsters. Often it was necessary to drive the cattle a mile or more from the corral in order to find sufficient grass, that near the road being kept short by the incoming trains from Mexico and the outgoing trains ahead of us.

At Council Grove there was a considerable settlement of Indian traders. There we found assembled a large band of Kaw Indians, who had just reached there from a buffalo hunt on the Arkansas. The Kaws were not classed as "wild" Indians, and I think had been assigned to a reservation not far off, but when they got off on a hunt their native savage inclinations made them about as dangerous as those roaming the plains at will, and whose contact with the white man was much less frequent.

Beyond the Diamond spring we met two men on horseback, who were hunting cattle belonging to a train then corralled some distance ahead. The cattle had been stampeded by Indians in the night and they had lost fifty head. The train could not be moved without them. The men had been in search of them for two days and thought they would be compelled to offer a reward for them, that being found necessary sometimes, along the border. The Indians and "squawmen"—white men married to, or living with, Indian squaws—would stampede cattle at night, drive them off and hold them until they ascertained that a reward had been offered for them. Then they would visit the corral, learn with seeming regret of the cause of the detention of the train, declare that they were well acquainted with the surrounding country and could probably find them and bring them in, offering to perform this service for so much a head. After the bargain was struck the cattle would be delivered as soon as they could be driven from the place of their secretion. It was not infrequent for a band of Kaws to strike a wagon master in this way for as much as from $100 to $500.

Here we learned that Colonel Albert Sidney Johnston, in command of a considerable force, had moved out from Fort Scott against the Cheyennes, who were on the warpath up on the Republican river, in the western part of Kansas, but we missed seeing the command until months later, on our homeward journey in September.

3

Buffalo

AS we were drawing near the buffalo range preparations were made for a chase. The pistols were freshly loaded and butcher knives sharpened. One morning about 9 o'clock, on Turkey creek, a branch of the Cottonwood, we came in sight of buffalo, in a great mass, stretching out over the prairie as far as the eye could reach, though the topography of the country enabled us to see for several miles in each direction. The prairie in front of us was gradually undulating, but offered no great hindrance to fast riding. Reece and I were anxious to try our skill, and Captain Chiles said he would go along to assist in butchering and bringing up the meat; but, as he was riding a mule, he could not be expected to take an active part in the chase. Reece was mounted on his splendid iron gray and I on my trained buffalo horse, each of us having a pair of Colt's navy revolvers, of six chambers in holsters.

We rode slowly until we got within three or four hundred yards of the edge of the vast herd. Then they began to run and we followed, gaining on them all the time. Pressing forward, at the full speed of my horse, I discovered that the whole band just in front of me were old bulls. I was so anxious to kill a buffalo that I began shooting at a very large one, occasionally knocking tufts of hair off his coat, but apparently having little other effect. However, after a lively run of perhaps a mile or two he slackened his pace and at last stopped still and, turning about, faced me. I fired the one or two remaining charges of my revolvers, at a distance of twenty or thirty yards, and thought he gave evidence of being mortally wounded. After gazing steadily at me for a few minutes he turned around and walked off. I followed, but presently he resumed a gallop in the direction the main herd had gone, soon disappearing from view over a ridge. So I had made a failure, and felt a good deal put out, as well as worn out by the fatigue of fast riding.

Through a vista between the clouds of dust raised by the buffalo, I got a glimpse of Reece. His horse proved to be very much afraid of the buffalo and could not be urged close enough to afford shooting, with any degree of certainty, with a pistol. Reece held his magnificent horse with a rein of the bridle in either hand, his head fronting towards the buffalo, but the frightened animal would turn to one side, despite the best efforts of his master, fairly flying around in front of the herd. That was Reece's first and last attempt to kill a buffalo on horseback.

I rode back towards the train, soon meeting Captain Chiles, who greeted me with derisive laughter, but considerately expressed the hope that I would have better success upon a second attempt. As we were all very anxious to get some fresh meat, he suggested that I should lend him my horse; that he would easily kill one with a double-barrel shotgun, which he was carrying in front on his saddle. I readily agreed to this, and mounting on my horse, he put off and promptly slew a fat, well-grown calf that proved good eating for us who had lived on bacon for many days.

That afternoon I turned my buffalo horse loose, permitting him to follow, or be driven along with the cavayard, in order that he might recuperate from the exhausting races of the forenoon. The following morning he was as good as ever, and I resolved to try another chase.

Having received some pertinent instructions from Captain Chiles, as to the modus operandi of killing buffalo on horseback at full speed, I mounted and sallied forth with him, the weather being ideal and the game abundant.

At the left of the road in sight, thousands of buffalo were grazing in a vast plain, lower than the ridge down which we were riding. Opened up in our view was a scope of country to the southeast of us, a distance of ten miles. This plain was covered with them, all heading towards the northwest.

At the outset I was more fortunate than on the previous day, for when I had gotten up close to them I found in front of me cows and calves, young things of one or two years old. Singling out a fat young cow, distinguished by her glossy coat of hair, I forced my horse right up against her and brought her down at the second shot. I pulled rein, stopping my horse as suddenly as was possible at the breakneck speed at which he was going, and in another moment the herd had spread out, and I was completely surrounded by the rushing mass of animals which my attack had set in motion.

The air was so clouded with dust that I could hardly see more than twenty yards from where I was standing, near the carcass of the cow I had killed. There was danger of being run over by them, but they separated as they approached, passing on either side of me, a few yards distant. After a while the rushing crowd thinned, and up rode Captain Chiles exclaiming: "Why don't you kill another?"

Fifty yards from us they were rushing by, all in the same direction. I again dashed into the midst of them, pressing my horse in pursuit of another young cow. She shot ahead of everything, increasing her speed so that I could hardly keep sight of her. While thus running at full speed my horse struck a calf with his breast, knocking the calf down flat, and almost throwing himself also. I pulled up as quickly as possible, turned around and shot the prostrate calf before it could get up. So I had two dead in, say twenty minutes. After this day's experience I had no trouble in killing all the buffalo we needed for our own consumption. For a week or ten days they were hardly out of sight. We found them as far west as Pawnee Rock. All told, I killed about twenty on the journey out and back. A good steak, cut from the loin of a buffalo cow, broiled on the coals with a thin slice of bacon attached to it to improve its flavor, was "good eating," and I soon became an accomplished broiler.

23

Companions of Voyage

BEFORE reaching Pawnee Rock we overtook a train of thirty wagons belonging to the leading freighters of the West, Majors, Russell & Waddell, with which we traveled to Fort Union, their freight being consigned to that post. This train had thirty wagons, built, I believe, in Philadelphia, with heavy iron axles and spindles, which seemed superior to any others I had seen on the prairie. Hagan was wagonmaster and Hines his assistant. The former was a sandy-haired man, who rode a large bay mule, a drowsy animal with immense lop ears that moved back and forth as he walked. This ungainly mule, I found out, in a day or two afterwards, had his good points. He could run as fast and get up as close to a buffalo as any horse in either outfit.

Notwithstanding Hagan's generally uncouth appearance, he was a man of sterling worth and a capital hand at killing buffalo. Subsequently we joined in many chases, and I found him an agreeable companion. On the rear end of each of the wagons in Hagan's train there was pasted a set of printed rules for the government of the employees in the service of Majors, Russell & Waddell. Both liquor and profanity were absolutely prohibited, but of the strict enforcement of the rules I cannot speak.

While riding in advance of the train, in company with Captain Chiles, we saw our Mexican friend, whose acquaintance we had formed at Westport, the master of his own train, galloping toward us, with a buffalo cow following close behind his horse. As was his habit, he had attacked the animal with his spear, stabbing her until she became infuriated so that she turned on him and was following him; it occurred to me she was pressing him a little too closely to be agreeable. We rode rapidly toward him, and as we were drawing near the cow became so exausted by loss of blood that she stopped still, when Captain Chiles rode up and gave her a broadside with his shotgun, which finished her.

Whenever they found buffalo in plenty the Mexicans would halt for several days and kill enough to supply their trainmen. They preserved the meat by cutting it into thin strips and hanging it on ropes about the corral until it was dried by the sun. But thus cured, it had a sour and disagreeable taste to me. The Mexicans would stew it with quantities of red pepper and devour it with great relish.

As we approached the valley of the Little Arkansas, where the view of the country was more extensive than any we had yet seen, there was no limit to the herds of buffalo, the face of the earth being covered with them. We camped at noon at the crossing of this stream. The buffalo were crossing the creek above us, moving westward, in bands of from twenty-five to a hundred or more. At the crossing they had a trail cut down through the steep banks of the stream three or four feet in depth.

But I had had enough of buffalo chasing, except when we were in need of fresh meat. It was too much like riding out into the pasture and killing your own domestic cattle. I found antelope hunting much better sport.

After Walnut creek, the next place of interest was Pawnee Rock* near which many battles between the traders and the Indians had taken place. This bluff, facing the road on the right hand side, at a distance, perhaps, of a hundred yards, was of brown sandstone about fifty feet high, the bluff end of the ridge extending down to the river bottom. I climbed up the almost perpendicular face of the elevation, where I found many names cut in the soft stone—names of Santa Fé traders who had traveled the trail, among them that of Colonel M. M. Marmaduke, who crossed to Mexico as early as 1826, and was afterwards governor of Missouri, and James H. Lucas, a prominent and wealthy citizen of St. Louis.

We were not particularly apprehensive of Indian troubles, although we knew the Cheyennes were turbulent. Elijah Chiles, a brother of our captain, had been loading goods at Kansas City when we left—a train of twenty-six wagons for the Kiowas and Comanches—and was doubtless a few day's drive behind us. But we kept on the lookout day and night; the guard around the cattle was doubled, and each teamster

*Pawnee Rock is in Barton County, central Kansas.

had a gun of some sort, which he kept strapped to the wagon bed, loaded and ready for service.

5

Pestiferous Indians

ALL the while we knew the Indians could wipe us out if they were determined to do so. In both trains there were not above sixty men, while there were, nearby, warriors by thousands. A day's journey beyond Pawnee Rock, we were visited by a hunting party of fifteen or twenty young Kiowa bucks, the first real "wild" Indians we had seen. They did not seem the least wild, however, but uncomfortably "tame," and disposed to get very familiar on short acquaintance. They were evidently out on a lark, and disposed to make us the objects of their amusement that afternoon.

They scattered up and down the length of both trains, talking and laughing with the teamsters. Two of them took particular fancy to my friend Reece, riding on either side of him, taking hold of his arms and seeming to admire his long hair and the handsome horse he rode. Reece was not at all afraid of them and permitted no undue interference with his person or property.

Reece was no coward. While we were still in the dangerous region, he would ride for miles ahead of the train, alone,
dismount and lie down to rest or sleep. When I said to him
that he was incurring unnecessary risk of being killed by the
Indians, he remarked that if they did kill him they could not
rob him of much in this world.

Along where we were traveling at the time of the visit of
the Kiowa bucks, the river bottom was as smooth as a billiard
table. Hagan's train was in the lead of ours a space of perhaps thirty yards intervening. Hagan and I were riding
abreast at the rear of his train, when suddenly, two of the
young bucks raised up a loud whoop and started their horses
at full speed. Taking a corner of their blankets in each hand
and holding them above their heads so that they made a flap-
ping sound in the air, they went sweeping along right against
the cattle, almost instantly creating a stampede, the cattle
turning out of the highway making the big wagons rattle
as they went.

For an instant Hagan sat on his mule stock still, apparently
dumbfounded. In another moment he put spurs to his mule,
intending to head the fleeing cattle. But instead of running,
the mule suddenly "bucked," throwing Hagan and his saddle
also (the girth breaking) over his head and landing him in
the road, flat on his back. Hagan got up, pulled himself together and rubbed the dust out of his eyes, but said nothing,
though gifted in the way of eloquent profanity.

No great harm resulted from the stampede. Some others
of the party of Indians ran ahead and stopped the cattle.

There was no collision of wagons and no damage, but the affair left an ugly feeling of resentment among the teamsters toward the Indians. The Indians laughed and talked about the affair among themselves. Any effort to punish them was out of the question, the entire tribes of Kiowas and Comanches being encamped within a day's journey above us.

The Indians kept along with the train all of the afternoon. Observing my horse and accoutrements, they inquired through Juan, the Spaniard, if he was fleet and good for buffalo, and pressed me to go out with them for buffalo the next day. I would gladly have seen the Indians engaged in a buffalo chase, but declined the invitation, making such excuses as I could without expressing any want of confidence as to their good fellowship. My scalp was intact and I felt disposed to keep it so.

The Kiowas begged Captain Chiles and Hagan to give them some flour and sugar, but they refused, knowing that a donation would be necessary later on, when we should meet the entire tribes of Kiowas and Comanches encamped above us, awaiting the arrival of their agent and the train load of goods for them.

Late in the evening, after we had corralled and the cooks were preparing to get supper these Indians having ridden off in the direction of the river, two of them reappeared. They returned to the camp, each with a bundle of dry driftwood, picked up on the river bank, which they threw down near the camp fire. This meant that they wanted supper, and Captain Chiles gave directions for the preparation of food for them. The Indians took supper with us, after which they departed, evidently feeling better and good naturedly disposed toward us.

That night there was much discussion of the Indian problem, with which we seemed now confronted. At noon the next day, as the cattle were being driven into the corral, another party of young warriors made their appearance at our camp, and came near involving us in a serious conflict. The trouble was brought on by the impatient action of our assistant wagonmaster, Rice. Four or five young fellows rode up into the rear entrance of our corral and were sitting there on their horses looking on at the yoking of the cattle. They partially blocked up the opening and interfered with egress of the teams. Rice, coming up behind them, without warning gave one of their horses a blow with a heavy blacksnake whip. The horse sprang forward, nearly unseating the rider, who, as soon as he could gather up the reins of his bridle, turned upon Rice in a towering rage, jerked an arrow from its quiver and fixed it in his bow. Forcing his horse right upon Rice, the Indian punched him with the point of the arrow until he knocked his hat off his head. Rice made no effort to resist the affront and threatened assault, but kept backing out of the Indian's reach.

I was standing near by and seized my pistol, thinking that a fight was imminent. At the height of the excitement, Captain Chiles made his appearance and commanded peace, in manner and language that the Indians could understand, but it required some time and a deal of talk to get them quieted. They denounced Rice's conduct as an insult they were bound to resent, and declared they would kill Rice sooner or later. Captain Chiles, speaking through Juan, our Spaniard, told them that if they commenced killing they would have to kill us all, for we were bound to stand together when it came to that. After a long wrangle the Indian said he would be satisfied if allowed to give Rice a sound flogging with a whip, but Captain Chiles refused. Finally the Indians seemed to recover their composure, to some extent, and rode off in the direction of the main camp.

Somewhere thereabout, in the river bottoms, I saw the ruins of an old adobe fort. "Old Fort Atkinson," doubtless named for and established and built by the command of Colonel Henry Atkinson of the regular army, with whose military career I happened to be somewhat familiar. The remains of the old fort excited my interest, but I do not recollect to have seen the place mentioned by any of the numerous accounts that have been written of the Santa Fé trail.

The fort was probably built in 1829. At that time a body of regular troops was sent out on the trail as a protection to the traders. Colonel Henry Atkinson was ordered west in 1818 and placed in command of the Ninth Military department, then comprising the entire country west of St. Louis, as well as Illinois and Wisconsin, with headquarters at Fort Bellefontaine, near St. Louis. He was soon afterward advanced in rank to brigadier general and held the command at Jefferson barracks until his death in 1842. The military post at Council Bluffs, Ia., was established by Colonel Atkinson in 1819, when he and his troops were transported on the first steamboats ascending the Missouri river. He served with distinction in the Black Hawk War, in command of the forces.

6

At the Kiowa Camp

THE train had got under way the next morning when the lodges of the Kiowas loomed up in sight of us. The camp seemed to extend over territory a mile square. The Indians said the entire tribe was assembled there—chiefs, warriors, squaws and papooses. Presently we could see them moving towards us, hundreds of them, on horseback and on foot, all sorts and sizes, men, women and children, coming to take a view of the white man and his belongings as they passed.

Soon we could see also the lodges of the Comanches, appearing about equal in number, and covering a like extent of country. The two camps were a mile or more apart.

It had been agreed between the wagonmasters that we would not make the usual noonday halt that day, but would drive by the Indian camps and as far beyond as it was possible for the cattle to stand the travel. We had anticipated a great throng of Indians, and here they came by the hundreds!

Some of the "big men" among them had guns or pistols, but the greater number, in fact almost every one, had a bow and quiver of arrows slung over his shoulders, even the children who looked not over ten years old. One chief wore a complete outfit of blue, with the insignia of a captain of the United States army, and had a Colt's revolver, but nearly all of them were naked to the waist, with a breech-clout and a sort of kilt of buckskin around the loins, hanging down nearly to the knees. Some wore moccasins, while many were barefooted.

The little fellows, nude, save for a breech-clout, had little bows about a foot long, with arrows of cactus thorn, with which they would shoot grasshoppers and other insects, showing astonishing skill. Numbers of the warriors carried spears, with long handles, glittering in the sunlight as they rode along, giving the caravan the appearance of a vast army of Crusaders on the march to the Holy Land.

Captain Chiles, endeavoring to shift the responsibility and escape the annoyance of the Indians, pointed to Reece, on his fine horse, and said: "There is the captain; talk to him. Ask him for what you want." But they could not be so easily deceived. It is said that you cannot fool Indians in this particular; that they never fail to distinguish the wagonmaster, and appear to select the chief of any crowd or caravan intuitively.

As we were traveling along the Indians gave frequent exhibitions of the speed of their horses, running races with each other, but at a sufficient distance not to frighten or stampede our cattle. The younger men kept up a continual chattering and laughing; horse racing seemed their great a-musement. The young fellows of the visit renewed their invitation, urging me to join them in a buffalo chase, explaining that the herds were not far off, and expressing a great desire to see a trial of my buffalo horse in a chase with theirs. I again declined. The train was continually moving and would not be stopped to suit my convenience, and there were other reasons, not unreasonably discreet.

The head men of the tribes, addressing the wagonmasters, complained that they were in great need of supplies, owing to the delay in the arrival of their annuities, and asked a gift from the two trains. The two wagonmasters, after some demurring, proposed to them that if they, with all their people, would withdraw from, and cease to follow the train, and desist from annoying us, after we had corralled, we would go into camp and give them such supplies as we could spare.

To this proposition the chiefs agreed. One of the leaders began talking in a loud voice to the multitude, gradually riding off from us, the crowd following. Reaching a knoll which elevated him so that he could overlook them, he dismounted and proceeded to make a speech. They seemed a little slow about leaving, the multitude appearing to be not altogether governed by the leaders, but nearly all finally withdrew in the direction of their own camp. Driving on a few hundred yards further, our corrals were formed and the cattle were driven off some distance for water, while preparations were made for cooking dinner.

In a little while the chiefs, representing both tribes, made their appearance at our corral, where the wagonmasters of both trains had met to hold the diplomatic conference to determine how much of a gift of supplies they were expecting from us.

The Indian chiefs dismounted from their horses, walked into the corral and sat down on the ground, in the semi-circle, to the number of perhaps a dozen and were soon joined by the wagonmasters, together with our interpreter Juan.

Writing now, in the year 1901, solely from memory, forty-three years since this scene occurred, I am unable to recollect all that was said, or the names of any of the Indians who were present and took part in this parley. No doubt San Tanta*, that famous Kiowa chief, was among them, but I took no notes whatever of this journey, and am forced now to rely entirely on my memory. I recall that it was stated that one of the most influential of the Comanche chiefs who was there was an out-and-out Spaniard or Mexican, speaking the Indian language as well as anybody, and was generally known and recognized as among the meanest, most cruel and blood thirsty of the Comanche tribe. One of the elder looking Indians produced a big pipe, filled it with tobacco, lighted it, and after taking a few puffs himself passed it to the one next to him. Thus the pipe was passed around to each one in the circle until all had taken part in the smoke. The Indians were dignified, discreet and cautious, as ap-

*Satanta, 1807(?)-1878.

peared to me during the conference, leaving the impression that our troubles with them were about to terminate, and this proved to be the fact.

At the close, and as a result of the council, a half-dozen sacks of flour, half that many sacks of sugar, and a lot of sides of bacon were brought forth from the mess wagons and stacked up on the ground, near where the collection of dignitaries of the prairies were sitting smoking the pipe of peace and good fellowship.

I thought the Indians regarded the things we were giving them, as a sort of tribute we were under obligations to pay for the privilege of passing through their country unmolested.

Pack mules were brought up, the supplies were loaded on them and they departed in the direction of the general camp, those engaged in the conference soon following.

In the evening, before we broke camp, two young bucks came galloping into the camp. Addressing Captain Chiles, they said that by instruction of their chief they had come to return a pair of blankets that had been stolen by one of the tribe. They threw down the blankets and the captain called to the men at the mess wagon to give them a cup of sugar each, saying that it was the first instance in his life when an Indian had restored stolen property.

7

To the Cimarron

ESCAPING any further delay from Indians or from other causes, good headway was made by the trains up the Arkansas until we reached the "lower crossing." It had been determined by the wagonmasters that we would cross the river here, taking the Cimarron route. Although the river was fordable, yet it was quite tedious and difficult to get the heavily loaded wagons across the stream, the water being waist-deep and the bottom uneven.

Neither an ox nor a mule will pull when he gets into water touching his body. The mule, under such circumstances, always has a tendency to fall down, and so get drowned, by becoming entangled in the harness. To meet this emergency the ox teams were doubled, ten yoke being hitched to each wagon, and were urged to do their duty by a half-dozen drivers on each side, wading through the water beside them.

The greater part of one day was taken up in getting the wagons across, but it was accomplished without serious loss. Everything being over, we encamped at the foot of the hill on the opposite side, and rested a day, in recognition of the Fourth of July. We fired some shots, and Captain Chiles brought forth from his trunk some jars of gooseberries, directing the cooks to make some pies, as an additional recognition of the national holiday. The gooseberries were all right, but the pie crust would have given an ostrich a case of indigestion.

The old Santa Fé trail, from the lower crossing of the Arkansas, ran southwest to the Cimarron, across a stretch of country where there was no water for a distance of nearly sixty miles, if my memory serves me correctly. All the water casks were filled from the Arkansas river for the use of the men, but of course there was no means of carrying water for horse or ox.

The weather was warm and dry, and now we were about to enter upon the "hornada,*" the Spanish word for "dry stretch." Intending to drive all night, starting was postponed until near sundown. Two or three miles from the Arkansas we apparently reached the general altitude of the plains over which we trudged during the whole night, with nothing but the rumbling of the wagons and the occasional shout of one of the drivers to break the silence of the plain.

It was my first experience of traveling at night, on this journey. Toward midnight I became so sleepy that I could hardly sit on my horse, so dismounting, I walked and led him. Advancing to a point near the head of the trains I ventured to lie down on the ground to rest, as the trains were

*Jornada; a day's journey, usually implying a difficult, often dry one.

passing at least. Instantly my clothes were perforated with cactus needles which pricked me severely, and waking me thoroughly. In the darkness it was with great difficulty I could get the needles out. Mounting my horse again I rode some distance in advance of everybody, completely out of hearing of the trains, and riding thus alone, with nothing visible but the stars, a feeling of melancholy seized me, together with a sense of homesickness, with which I had not hitherto been troubled. Each day's travel was increasing the distance between me, my home and my mother, to whom I was most dearly attached; and here amid the solitude, darkness and perfect quietude of the vast plains I began to reflect upon the dangers besetting me, and the uncertainty of ever returning to my home or seeing my relatives again.

The approach of morning and the rising of the sun soon dispelled these forebodings of evil and revived my spirits. Old Sol, like a ball of fire, emerged from the endless plain to the east of us, as from the ocean, soon overwhelming us with a flood of light such as I had never experienced before. During all that day's march the heat was intense and the sunlight almost blinding, the kind of weather that creates the mirage of the plains. In the distance on either hand, fine lakes of clear water were seen glistening in the sun, sometimes appearing circular in shape, surrounded with the proper shores, the illusion being apparently complete, so much so that several times during the day I rode some distance seeking to ascertain if they were really lakes or not. I found them receding as I approached, and was unable to get any closer to them than when as a boy I set out to find the sack of gold at the end of the rainbow.

About midday we passed a great pile of bleached bones of mules that had been thrown up in a conical shaped heap by the passing trainmen, in the course of the ten years they had been lying there. They were the remains of 200 or 300 mules belonging to John S. Jones, a Missourian, a citizen of Pettis county,* whom I knew personally. In 1847, and for many years afterward, Jones was engaged in freighting a-cross the plains. In '47, having obtained a contract from the government to transport freight for the troops at Santa Fé, he got a start late in the season, and had only reached the crossing of the Arkansas when he was overtaken by such deep snow and severely cold weather as to compel him to stop and go into quasi-winter quarters. While there, pro-tected by such barracks for man and beast as could be hast-ily constructed, he received orders from the commander of the troops in New Mexico that he must hurry up with the supplies, orders of such urgency that they could not be dis-regarded. He had a mule train of thirty wagons. Orders were given to hitch up and start. The weather moderated the first day, but on the second they encountered a heavy and cold rain freezing as it fell, and were forced to go into corral. Intense cold followed and every one of the mules froze to death, huddling in the corral, during the night. Years afterwards, through the influence of Colonel Benton in the Senate and John G. Miller of Missouri in the House of

*The county south of Saline County.

Representatives an appropriation was made by Congress of $40,000 to pay Mr. Jones for the loss of his mules.

In the forenoon of the second day from the Arkansas we reached Sand creek, a tributary of the Cimarron, where we found a pool of stagnant water, not enough for the oxen, but sufficient for the trainmen to make coffee with, and there we camped. A few hours afterwards we struck the valley of the Cimarron, and, after riding up the bed of the apparently dry stream, we discovered a pool of clear water. The cattle were so famished that they ran into it, hitched to the wagons, their drivers being unable to restrain them, and it was with considerable difficulty that the wagons were afterwards pulled out of the mud.

8

My First Antelope

AFTER reaching the Cimarron we began seeing herds of antelope in the distance. At first I tried "flagging" them. I had been told that on approaching within two or three hundred yards of them, concealed from their view behind an intervening ridge, these animals were possessed of such inordinate curiosity that they could be enticed to within gunshot of the hunter by tying a handkerchief on the end of a stick and elevating it in sight of the antelope, the hunter, of course, keeping concealed. I made several efforts at this plan of exciting their curiosity, and while some of them came toward me at first sight of the flag, their curiosity seemed counterbalanced by caution or incredulity, and in no instance could I get one to come near enough for a sure or safe shot. I then tried a rifle, with which I was also unsuccessful, not then being able to make a correct estimate of the distance between me and the antelope, a troublesome task, only to be acquired by experience and constant practice.

The old trail ran along up the valley of the Cimarron

several days' drive. A singular stream was the Cimarron; for the most part of the bed of the stream was sand, perfectly dry, but now and then, every mile or two, we found a hole of clear good water, except that it was slightly tinctured with alkali, a brackish, but not unpleasant taste. There were three fairly good springs along the road near the Cimarron, designated as the lower, middle and upper spring, and we camped near each of them as we passed. As we traveled up the valley squads of antelope could be seen viewing the train from the heights on either side of the valley.

Captain Chiles had along with him two shotguns, the smaller he had been using on buffalo, the other, an unusually large, double barrel, number 8 bore, very long in barrel and heavy, carrying easily twenty buckshot in each barrel. Armed with that big gun I would ride in the direction of the antelope, but at an angle indicating that I would pass them. Usually when I had gotten within three or four hundred yards of them they would quietly withdraw from view behind the ridge, whereat, I would turn the course of my horse and gallop as fast as I could, keeping the ridge between them and me until I had gotten within a short distance of the point of their disappearance. Then dismounting, I hastily followed them on foot. Often they would be found to have moved not out of the range of that big gun, and with it I killed many of them. That was the only plan of killing antelope by which I gained success. During this part of the journey we saw many wolves, and of many varieties, from the little coyote to the great gray wolf. They were all very shy, however, and difficult to approach within gun shot.

On the Cimarron we were overtaken by the mail coach, one of the monthly lines then operated by Waldo & Co.° of Independence, Mo. The coach had left Westport five days later than our train. The driver, guards and passengers were all "loaded to the guards" (to use a steamboat phrase) with guns and pistols.

While the train was under headway one morning Captain Chiles rode along the length of the train inquiring for "Skeesicks," but "Skeesicks" did not answer, and no one could tell anything about him. The captain ordered the train stopped and a search to be made of each wagon, but the searchers failed to find any sign of "Skeesicks." Further inquiry developed the fact that he had started out as one of the guards at midnight to protect the herd of cattle, they being off a mile or more from the corral, where grass was found, and no one had seen him since. Captain Chiles declared that he could not afford to stop for so worthless a fellow as "Skeesicks," and thereupon the orders were given for the train to proceed.

Having traveled ten or twelve miles, a camp was located at the foot of a mound which overlooked the road we had been traveling for nearly the whole distance of the morning's drive.

At dinner, the propriety of laying by for a day or two, or long enough to make a proper search for our lost comrade,

---

°Owned by Dr. David Waldo (1802-1878), who made a fortune in the early Santa Fé trade.

was discussed; but the teamsters all realized that no captain of a ship at sea ever wielded more absolute authority than Captain Chiles. He could brook no oppositon, and little criticism of his course or conduct. Any disobedience of his orders he regarded as equal to mutiny and was punished accordingly. About the entire camp a sullen silence prevailed. Suddenly some one cried out that an object could be seen away down the road that might be "Skeesicks," but just then, no one could discern whether a man or a horse or an Indian.

The entire party assembled outside the corral to watch the approaching object, and after a while our lost "Skeesicks" walked up, covered with dust and worn out with fatigue of constant walking for over twelve hours, without food or water.

He was soon revived by a comforting dinner. He said he had been aroused at midnight from a sound sleep to assume his turn as cattle guard, and on his way from the corral to the herd, he had wandered apart from his companion guard, soon becoming bewildered and completely lost. He wandered about during the entire night, not knowing in what direction he was going, and was all the while afraid to stop for fear of the wolves that were howling around him continually. After daylight he accidentally found the road, and although bewildered, he had sense enough remaining to follow it to the west, whence he had overtaken us.

As the cattle were being yoked, Captain Chiles called up "Little Breech" and directed him to get the large cow bell he had brought along to put on the black steer that was in the habit of wandering from the herd at night. The wagon-master, with the bell in hand, walked up to "Skeesicks," who was sitting on a wagon tongue resting his weary legs, and said, " 'Skeesicks,' I am determined not to lose you again, and am going to take no chances." Then he buckled the strap attached to the bell around "Skeesick's" neck. Turning to "Little Breech" he gave him particular orders to drive "Skeesicks" in the cavayard and in no event to allow him to wander away again.

All that afternoon "Skeesicks" plodded along with the lame cattle in the cavayard, at the rear of the train, the bell ringing at every step. In the evening, after we had cor-ralled, he went to Captain Chiles and plaintively beseeched him to remove the bell. The captain gently unbuckled the strap, but again charged "Little Breech" to keep his eye on "Skeesicks" and not permit him to wander from the train.

9

A Kicking Gun
And a Bucking Mule

HERE for some days we were traversing a continuous level plain, treeless and trackless, except for the road we traveled, covered with buffalo grass, then turned a beautiful straw color by the sun and dry weather, but still affording excellent pasturage. Not a tree had we seen, none since we crossed the Arkansas.

We were slowly but regularly leaving behind us the monotonous plain, to enter upon a region of great natural beauty and attractiveness. On a beautiful morning after the train had been moving for a short time, the Rabbit Ear mounds were seen, peering up in the distance, through the hazy atmosphere. Yet we were a day's journey from them. These twin diminutive sentinels of the Rockies, stationed here to the left of our road, could not have been more appropriately named, their resemblance to the ears of a jack-rabbit being strikingly obvious.

A day or two after passing the Rabbit Ears* we were fortunate in the beauty and attractiveness of the location of our corral. Immediately west of us the view was limited to a mile or two, shut off by the bluff rim of a stretch of table-land, rising perhaps a hundred feet above our level, the face of the elevation extending north and south, the road we were traveling passing around the base of its southern extremity. About midway of the rim of this plateau of table-land there was a small mound of regular sugar-loaf shape, rising to perhaps the height of twenty feet, on the top pinnacle of which stood a single buck antelope looking at the train as it was starting out just at sunrise. There he stood for some time stock still gazing at us. The morning was absolutely glorious, the perfect weather of New Mexico. I determined to give this solitary buck antelope a trial.

Procuring the big double-barreled shotgun belonging to Captain Chiles, I mounted my horse, riding in almost the opposite direction to that in which the train was moving. The buck held his position until I had ridden nearly opposite him, my course, leaving him nearly half a mile to the left, when he suddenly retired behind the mound. Immediately turning my horse I galloped over the ascending ground until I got within a hundred yards of the base of the mound, dismounted quickly, walked rapidly up to it; then I crawled as quietly as possible nearly to the top. Peeping around so as to get a view of the opposite side, I beheld, forty yards from me, that fine buck, looking intently toward me, with four or

*Rabbit Ear Mountains, in Union County, northeastern New Mexico.

📖 50

five of his companions lying down near him, so close together that I could almost have covered them all with the big shotgun.

Holding the gun in the right hand—it was so heavy that I could scarcely handle it—cocking both barrels, I pushed it out in front of me, and just as I was in the act of placing the breech of the gun against my shoulder, but before I had gotten it fairly in place, off it went, both barrels simultaneously, sounding like a cannon, and kicking me with such force as to turn me over and over, rolling me down nearly to the foot of the mound. The gun struck my face, bruising it badly, making my nose bleed profusely and stunning me, but not so badly but that I noticed the bunch of fine antelope scampering off, frightened, but untouched. My horse stood quietly where I had left him picketed.

Our real character, "Little Breeches," antedated the poetical child of the fancy of Colonel John Hay,[*] introduced to the public some thirty years ago. Whether this distinguished gentleman had any knowledge of our cavayard driver, I do not know, but in truth the two "Little Breeches" had similar characteristics, both "chawing tebacker" at an early age, and our "Little Breeches" had the additional accomplishment of swearing with emphasis, and articulation unexcelled or unequaled by any of the older and more hardened "bull-whackers" of our train.

"Little Breech" rode a pony mule, a small animal of most

---

[*]Reference is to John M. Hay, scholar and statesman (1838-1905), author of *Pike County Ballads*, Boston, 1871.

perfect shape, with activity to correspond. The noon-day camp was breaking up, the cattle were all yoked and hitched to the wagons. "Little Breech" had mounted his mule, preparing to round up his cavayard. At the moment the reins were lying loose on the mule's neck, while "Little Breech" had both hands employed in adjusting his belt. Impulse dictated so, walking towards him unobserved, I picked up a stick, raised the mule's tail and gently placed the stick under it. The mule instantly clasped it tight with his tail, commencing, before "Little Breech" could seize the bridle reins, the worst spell of bucking I had witnessed on the journey. He jumped and kicked and kicked and jumped for a hundred yards, describing a semi-circle in his gyrations. I was alarmed, fearing the boy's neck would surely be broken. But failing to get hold of the bridle reins, he clamped the horn of the Spanish saddle, and, retaining his seat to the end, all the while swearing at me with as great force as he could command, his volubility being very much restricted by the prolonged bucking.

10

A Gray Wolf

IT IS difficult, if not impossible, to find the derivation of some of the Spanish or Mexican words and phrases then in use by the Santa Fé traders. For instance the word "cavayard," I have used and spelled as it was pronounced by these unlettered plainsmen and as applied by them to the bunch of loose cattle and horses driven behind the train. The pure Castilian has undoubtedly suffered many changes in New Mexico, among the lower classes particularly. The Spanish words used by these plainsmen had been both Mexicanized and then Missourianized until so changed and corrupted as to be hardly recognizable at all. This word "cavayard," they declared, was of Spanish origin; if so it must have been a corruption of "caballar"—pronounced "cavallyar," meaning an attendant on horses. The derivation of the word "hornada," which we found given to the dry stretch between the Arkansas and Cimarron is equally obscure.

Among the teamsters was a Mexican, whose name I have forgotten. One morning Captain Chiles got up earlier than usual, at break of day, in fact, and, while waking up the men, he discovered this Mexican beating one of his oxen severely with bow of the ox yoke. This was a gross violation of the rules, but when Captain Chiles censured him in pretty strong language he talked back to him in a threatening manner. Thereupon the captain, drawing one of the two navy pistols swinging to a belt around his waist, holding it in one hand, and with a heavy blacksnake whip in the other, advanced upon him and proceeded to give him a severe flogging with the whip. The Mexican was held fast by the threatening aspects of the navy pistol pointed at him all the while until he had received a very severe flogging. The following night the Mexican "skipped out" and was never seen by us afterwards, but no doubt made his way to the settlements of New Mexico, then not more than 200 miles distant.

Hunting game, other than buffalo, along the Santa Fé trail at that date was, to one attached to a train and dependent upon its movements, necessarily confined to a narrow scope of country on either side of the road, within a mile or two. It was impossible to know at what moment one might meet with Indians and be attacked by them. At that time of the year the game was kept back from the highway by the frequent passage of trains, while a few miles off from the road there was no trouble to find antelope and white-tail deer. I was compelled to hunt alone or not at all. My friend Reece had become too much worn out by the travel and his continued ill health to take much interest in hunting, while Captain Chiles was kept busy with his duties about the train. But I was continually on the lookout for game; I rarely traveled the road, but would ride a mile or so from it on one side or the other, always carrying my holster pistols, and usually, in addition the big shotgun belonging to Captain Chiles.

My buffalo horse seemed to have a very clear understanding of travel over the plains, having, as before stated, the experience of a journey from California to Missouri the previous year. He seemed to have an instinctive idea of the locality of the train, even when it was traveling, and often when riding him a mile or more from the road and completely out of sight, when given the rein he would instantly change his course in the proper direction to intercept the train.

Riding thus alone on one occasion, some distance ahead of the train, I saw a large gray wolf galloping across my course, going towards the road. I determined to give him a chase, and after him I went. The wolf increased his speed, and, urging my horse to his best, we went flying across the road 100 yards in front of the train and in full view of it. As we flew by, the entire company of teamsters gave us an encouraging whoop, but whether designed for me or the wolf I was not able to determine. I had followed the big fellow closely for a mile, emptying at him, if not in him, the entire twelve chambers of my revolvers. At one time I got within twenty feet of him, but not having any ammunition for reloading with me, nor time for recharging my pistols if I had, he disappeared over the ridge and I saw nothing more of him.

Many days passed and many weary miles were traveled of which I have no remembrance whatever and I am only attempting to relate such adventures as were indelibly impressed upon my memory, the frosts of forty-three winters having passed over my head since this journey was made. I cannot recollect what I thought of the probability of those vast plains ever being occupied or cultivated as homes for white people.

Whetstone creek, which the road crossed near the boundary of New Mexico, was one of the localities of special interest to me. Back on my father's farm in Missouri I had often whetted my pocketknife on a stone belonging to my old overseer friend who said he had obtained it on this creek. But none of our trainmen were familiar with the route or the locality, or could tell me where the whetstone quarry was to be found, and I was disappointed in not being able to discover it after making a diligent search for it. And now the spurs of the Raton mountains loomed up in the distance ahead of us, a novel and interesting sight to many of the company, some of whom had never seen any greater elevation than the big hills of Western Missouri, and the drivers swore and cracked their whips with renewed vigor and animation.

11

Arrival at Las Vegas

CROSSING the Ocata* on the dry bed of it we were approaching Apache hill, on the branch of the road leading to Fort Union, the ascent of which was quite difficult to heavily loaded wagons. The hill was barely visible in the distance and the hour nearly noon when we first came in sight of it. It was quite hot under the noonday sun and we could see the white sheets of a train of wagons descending the hill. Soon afterwards Captain Chiles and I, riding ahead of our train, met the wagonmaster of this train, a sandy-haired, red-faced fellow, sullen, morose and non-communicative. He seemed inclined to pass us without speaking, but Captain Chiles saluted him, and he halted for a few moments. The man appeared to be sick, and as Captain Chiles afterwards said he could scarcely "pull a word out of him with a log chain."

The captain asked him, "How is the grass about the foot

*Ocaté crossing.

of Apache hill?" when he answered, "Well, sir, it's damned scase."

Ten miles before reaching Fort Union we stopped at a ranch, where we found an abundance of good milk and butter, kept in a well arranged spring house, supplied with water by a cold and bold spring running out of the foot of the mountain. The milk was kept in large open tin pans, set in a ditch extending around the room, constructed so as to allow a continual flow of cool water about the pans. The spring house was built of adobe or sod bricks. This ranch supplied the fort with milk and butter.

Fort Union* had no appearance of a fortified place then; there was nothing more than substantial and comfortable barracks, stores and warehouses. But the place had a look of military precision, neatness and cleanliness about it not seen elsewhere in New Mexico.

At this place our train was cut in twain; one-half of it, under the command of Captain Chiles went on to Mora, the other half was sent to Las Vegas, in charge of the assistant wagonmaster, Rice. Reece and I decided to accompany that part going to Las Vegas.

On the route to Las Vegas we found a large adobe ranch house, probably a hundred feet square and sixteen feet high, the solid walls being without openings on the outside, except two large doors. The ventilation and light were secured through the openings inside the hollow square. There was an extensive buckskin tailoring establishment there, where

*Now a National Monument in Mora County.

📖 58

they were manufacturing quantities of buckskin clothes of various patterns, and I was surprised at the skill displayed in making the garments. The clothes were made to fit with tailor-like precision and exactness. Clothes of buckskin were generally worn at that time by the inhabitants of New Mexico, by the natives especially.

As we drew near Las Vegas we noted that the "bottoms" of the little creek running near the town were cultivated in corn, with occasional patches of vegetables, the land unenclosed by fences, but flanked by irrigating ditches supplying the necessary water, and the crops were looking remarkably well, although the weather had been dry for some weeks. We found it necessary to have a close watch kept on our cattle while we were near these cultivated and unfenced fields. Las Vegas was a compactly built little town of probably two or three hundred inhabitants, the houses for the most part built of adobe bricks or tufts of sod, with a corral in the rear. The herds of sheep, goats and burros were driven in about sunset and fastened up for the night in these corrals, from which they were driven out early in the morning to graze during the day, under the constant eye of the herder, who accompanied each band.

We remained one day only at Las Vegas. The wagons were unloaded, the freight being delivered to the consignees, and we turned about and started on our homeward journey.

While at Las Vegas Reece purchased three goats, thinking that their milk would be beneficial to him. They furnished a bountiful supply of milk, and very rich milk it was, too, though of a rather strong and disagreeable taste and odor. He failed, however, to realize any great benefit from its use, so far as I remember.

Our first noonday camp after we left Las Vegas was near a ranch, and as we were resting under the shade of the wagons after dinner, the owner of the ranch, a native New Mexican, visited us, with a good looking shepherd dog following him. Reece expressed admiration for this dog, which, the Mexican declared, was excellently well trained for herding, easily controlled and a valuable animal in other respects. After considerable negotiation, the Mexican agreed to sell the dog to Reece for two plugs of tobacco. Reece procured a rope, and the Mexican tied the dog to the rear axle of one of the freight wagons, soon afterward taking his departure for his ranch a mile or more distant. Shortly the dog became restless and made efforts to get loose.

The teamsters began to laugh at Reece about the uncertain character of his newly acquired property, saying that the Mexican well knew that he could not keep the dog, and that he would soon make his escape to return home. Reece declared that he would prevent this at least and went to a wagon and brought forth a gun. Standing the gun against the wagon under which the dog was fastened, Reece resumed his efforts to enjoy a noonday siesta under a neighboring wagon. He was aroused by one of the drivers, who shouted to him that his dog was running off in the direction of his home. The dog had gotten two or three hundred yards away, ascending a ridge in a gallop when Reece jumped up, seized the gun, leveled it at the dog and fired. To his surprise, no less than ours, the dog fell dead.

We rejoined the other part of the train at a camp near Fort Union, and here in this camp we remained for several days.

Captain Chiles was desirous of selling a part of the cattle, as the whole were not needed to convey the empty wagons on the return journey, and made frequent visits to the fort in his efforts to dispose of the cattle. One evening he announced that he had made a sale of about one-half of the cattle. The following morning a prosperous looking gentleman of consequential air and mien rode up to our camp and was introduced as the purchaser of our cattle. He was riding a fine horse, with saddle and other equipment to correspond. Among his other attractive features, I can recollect a large flask of brandy which he carried lashed to the front of his saddle, the flask being protected by a wicker jacket. Generous gentleman, as he proved, the first thing he said after the usual salutation was an invitation to sample the contents of this flask, and this invitation the common politeness of the plains prevented us from declining. We found his brandy excellent, and its effect produced a lasting remembrance of the personality of the gentleman himself.

The cattle purchased by him were cut out and separated from the others. The owner said he intended driving them to some point in New Mexico, a considerable distance from there. On inquiring for some hands whom he could employ to drive them to their destination, one or two were found in the party who would accept the service offered, and then some one suggested that a job of this sort would suit "Skeesicks," who was still hanging to the train.

"Skeesicks," with apparent reluctance, accepted the service and wages offered, and in a few moments afterwards left us forever. I could not avoid feeling sorry for him, as he slowly passed from our view, trudging along on foot behind the herd of cattle. We never heard of him afterwards.

While at this camp a Mexican youth, about 16 years of age, came to the train and asked permission to accompany us to the "States." He was a bright, active boy, able to understand and speak English in some degree, appearing immensely pleased when Captain Chiles told him that he might come along with us if he desired.

During the night some of the trainmen ascertained that he was a "peon," consequently having no right to leave the territory. When the train started the next morning, at the suggestion of the men, he secreted himself in one of the covered wagons. Before noon, however, two horsemen were seen following us, coming on in a fast gallop. They were officers of the law, armed with pistols and a writ for the arrest of the boy. The trainmen pretended to be ignorant of his presence with the train, but the officers said they knew he was with the train, demanding of Captain Chiles that he stop the train so they might search for him. In order to avoid being subjected to the charge of resisting the officers, the captain ordered a halt. The officers soon discovered the boy concealed beneath some bedding, dragged him out and put him on one of their horses. The poor boy protested with all his might against being taken back, crying all the while in a distressing manner, arousing the feelings of the trainmen until they were about to declare war on the officers, but Captain Chiles said it would not do to resist the civil authorities. So the little fellow was carried back to his condition of slavery or peonage as it was called by the officers.

At noon that day our camp was near the base of a mound of broken rock, perhaps a hundred feet high, rounded to a sharp pinnacle at its apex. The mound supported hardly a bit of vegetation on its sides which were nearly inaccessible. The goats purchased by Reece had been driven along in the cavayard, apparently reconciled to their new mode of life and daily travel. That day, as the wagons were moving out of corral, Reece missed his goats. I joined him in a search for them, riding about over the plain, and we had about reached the conclusion that they had run away. Just then as the wagons were moving from the corral one of the teamsters shouted to Reece, "There are your goats!" pointing to the summit of the steep mound of rock.

Sure enough, there were the three goats, standing in a row on the topmost rock, looking at us with the utmost satisfaction and composure. Nothing but a goat could either ascend or descend the declivity, so Reece and I remained until they thought proper to come down. This they did in the course of an hour, when we drove them on, overtaking the train as it went into camp at nightfall.

12

In Peril of Indians

THE return journey was for the most part uneventful, but with empty wagons we could travel more rapidly. On our reaching the crossing of the Arkansas we found there a company of dragoons, and the officers informed us that they had been fighting and chasing the Cheyennes all summer, having just halted there in following one band of these Indians to the Arkansas river. They had been forced to abandon their provision wagons some days before we saw them, and were almost entirely out of food. The artillery had also been left behind two or three day's march down the Arkansas river. These troops, a part of Colonel Sumner's regiment, had had several brushes with the Cheyennes, and captured a lot of horses from the Indians. The soldiers, their horses and equipments, gave every evidence of having undergone a severe campaign, and they came around our camp begging for something to eat, tobacco and whisky, much as the Indians were in the habit of doing. But our ability to relieve their wants was very limited, having with us only supplies enough for our own party back to the settlements.

The officers said that it would be hazardous for us to proceed further, advising our captain to remain until the trains in our rear could get up, until they had accumulated to at least one hundred wagons and men, when we would be strong enough to resist any attack that we were likely to be subjected to.

Acting on this advice, we remained in camp several days, until five or six trains had arrived and camped in our immediate vicinity. The journey was then resumed, our train taking the lead, all our weapons of defense being put in as good order as possible. After the trains were under way the wagonmasters of those behind us, to the number of ten or a dozen, mounted on horses and mules, would ride ahead to join Captain Chiles, Reece and myself, thus forming a lively and agreeable company of companionable men.

As we were thus riding along down the level bottom of the Arkansas, some distance in advance of the trains away to our right a mile or more, out near the bank of the river, where we could see some scattering cottonwood trees, we observed a smoke rising from a camp fire. Some one of the party suggested that it was the smoke of the camp of the artillery company, of which we had been told, so we rode forward, giving little more attention to the smoke of the camp fire that went curling upward among the cottonwood. When we had reached a point about opposite the smoke there suddenly appeared in our view a company of some

65 ꜩ

fifty horsemen, riding pell-mell in a fast gallop towards us. They were yet too far off to be distinctly seen or for us to tell what manner of men they were. In another moment, Captain Chiles exclaimed:

"Men, they are Indians! Soldiers don't ride in that disorderly manner. Form a line and get out your guns. We are in for it!"

Instantly all hands obeyed his command, forming a line facing the enemy, each of us drawing a pistol. The lead wagons of our train were just barely visible, probably two miles from us. When the approaching horsemen saw that we had formed a line of battle, they instantly drew rein, slackening their speed to a walk, but kept steadily drawing nearer us.

In a few minutes our anxiety was relieved when these horsemen came near enough for us to see that they were white men, not Indians, and, after all, they proved to be the company of artillery, mounted on some Indian horses that had lately been captured from the Cheyennes. Under the circumstances it was not at all strange that we had mistaken them for hostile Indians.

The next morning after this the wagonmasters of these several trains came forward as usual, and we set out to travel in advance of the trains, hoping to find buffalo, as we had again reached their accustomed range.

I had the only real good buffalo horse in the company, but his speed and strength we found considerably lessened and impaired by the long journey. In discussing the prospects of finding buffalo, and of killing one for a supply of fresh meat, which we were all very eager again to get, Hines, an assistant wagonmaster of one of the trains, suggested to me that I should use his pair of heavy Colt's army revolvers, which, he said, carried a heavier ball and were more effective in killing buffalo than mine. Although I was somewhat doubtful, I exchanged with him. We had ridden forward but a few miles when we descried a herd of some twenty buffalo, in the distance. The understanding being that I was to lead off in this chase, I put spurs to my horse, the others following. There were several young cows in the band, one of which I selected, and pressed my horse forwards. In a few moments we were going at a furious rate of speed, and my prospect of success was good, but just as I was leaning forward, with pistol in my right hand in the act of shooting the cow, the stirrup leather of my saddle suddenly broke, almost precipitating me headlong to the ground, but I escaped falling by catching around the horse's neck with my left arm; the heavy pistol fell to the ground. While I was preparing to mend the stirrup leather, having dismounted for that purpose, the other men of the party rode up, the buffalo, meanwhile, having run entirely out of sight.

When I had gotten the stirrup repaired, Captain Chiles noticing that I was a good deal shaken up and unnerved by the occurrence, said that I would better let him have my horse and pistols, which I readily gave up to him, knowing that there was no man on the plains who excelled him in a

67 ✍

buffalo chase or one more sure to provide fresh meat. So he mounted my horse, and I got upon his mule, and we all started off in the direction the buffalo had gone. We had by that time reached a section of rolling country on the "cut-off" across the bend of the Arkansas, lying in great ridges, with valleys intervening. As we got to the top of one of these ridges Captain Chiles, who was in front, exclaimed: "Look yonder at that band of elk!"

There they were, perhaps two hundred of them, grazing in a valley a mile distant. I immediately claimed my horse, for I did not want to miss the opportunity of killing an elk, but the captain merely laughed at me and started down toward the elk in a gallop. The elk, seeing him, were soon all in motion, running in a great mass, stirring up a cloud of dust, soon passing from our view around the point of the ridge on the farther side of the valley, Captain Chiles following them closely, the horse at full speed. After they had gotten out of sight of us we heard the report of his pistol, two or three times, and our entire party followed in his wake until we had reached the point, where we thought the firing had occurred. Finding neither Chiles nor any dead or wounded elk the men all, except Reece and I, refused to go further, and turned about towards the road. Reece, who was riding his big gray horse, and I, on the mule, continued riding in the direction we supposed Chiles had gone, until we had ridden perhaps four miles, when I began to feel a little uneasy, expressing a disinclination to go further, as I was riding a worn-out, leg-weary mule, with nothing but a belt pistol in the way of arms, and being in the neighborhood of hostile Indians. Reece said to me: "You remain here while I ride to the top of that high mound yonder," pointing to a hill a mile farther on. "When I get there," he said, "if then I can neither hear nor see anything of Chiles or the elk I will return here for you."

Reece rode away. I remained alone for an hour or more —the danger of the situation made it appear much longer than it really was, no doubt—and finally I saw Reece and Chiles coming, greatly to my relief. They were in good spirits, and as they rode up Chiles said they had killed the biggest elk that ever ran on the plains, giving me an account of his capture in detail as we rode back.

13

Captain Chiles' Chase

WHEN Reese had got to the top of the mound he saw Captain Chiles, sitting on a horse, holding by a rope a huge bull elk. The elk stood in the bottom of a deep, narrow ditch, ten feet deep, with banks almost perpendicular, so steep that he was unable to get up them or out of the ditch to assail his captor. Captain Chiles, when he first caught up with the band of elk, had made an effort to kill one with the pistols, but for some reason he could only get the pistols to fire two of the charges, and with these two he only wounded a cow slightly, not enough to to stop her from running. He kept after the band, all the while trying to get the revolver to fire, trying every chamber, but with no success. After he had kept up the chase for two or three miles the large bull elk, being very fat, got too tired to keep up with the band, but trotted along behind, in fact, so far exhausted that Chiles could keep up with him with his horse in a trot. The captain despaired of being able to stop one with the pistols, and, finding a small lariat I had brought from the Kiowas as we went out, on my saddle, used for picketing my horse, resolved to try the plan of lassoing the big fellow.

Being an expert in rope throwing, he had little difficulty in preparing the noose or getting a fastening around the top prong of one branch of the elk's great antlers. As soon as the elk found he was restrained by the rope he turned about and charged on Captain Chiles with all the power and fury he could command, and twice or thrice the captain was forced to cut loose from him in order to escape his assaults. The rope was long enough to drag on the ground some distance behind him, so that the captain could recover hold of it without dismounting, reaching down and picking it up as the bull trotted away from him. He kept on after him for some distance, occasionally jerking him back, and worrying him until he could hardly walk. Coming to the lower end of the ditch, washed out to a depth of ten feet, at a point a few yards above, he managed to guide the animal, bewildered as he was by the heat, together with the violent and prolonged exercise, into it, leading or driving him along up the ditch until he got him in between the high banks of it to a place where the animal could not get at him however anxious he was to do so.

When Reece arrived, as above related, he found Chiles sitting there on the horse holding the end of the rope, but having nothing with which to kill the animal, not even a pocket pistol. Reece had with him a belt revolver, and, under the directions of Chiles, he carefully crawled to the edge of the ditch to within a few feet of the elk's head and killed him with a couple of shots in the forehead.

The bull had not been wounded by Chiles, and no one but a veritable daredevil as he was would have undertaken the job of lassoing an elk under such circumstances as he did. But Chiles was a stranger to fear.

Chiles, Reece and I got to the camp about 2 o'clock, near six miles from where the elk was killed. After dinner we went out with pack mules and the necessary hatchets and butcher knives, and two of the drivers, to butcher the elk. The animal was a splendid specimen of his kind, supporting a magnificent pair of antlers, fully hardened and developed, and was fatter than any other animal of the deer kind I have seen, before or since. We butchered and brought to camp on the pack mules every part of his carcass, including the antlers. The latter were brought home to Jackson county.* We feasted on the flesh of the fat elk for several days, and my recollection is that I never tasted better meat.

The remaining part of the journey was uneventful, the entire party remaining with the train until we were within eighty miles of the state line of Missouri. Then, in company with Captain Chiles, I started, before daylight, to make a forced march to Westport. We rode forty miles before we halted for breakfast, obtaining it at a settler's cabin in the vicinity of Black Jack, arriving in Westport late in the eve-

*Independence and modern Kansas City are in Jackson County, one of the westernmost counties of Missouri.

ning, in the latter part of September, feeling very willing to rest once more in a comfortable house and bed.

I saw my friend Reece about a year after he had returned to his home in Missouri still making a fight for life, but during the second year he struck his flag and made a final surrender.

At Westport the drivers were paid off and disbanded, but I was not present to witness the separation of the company that had formed a companionship, offensive and defensive, during this long and tiresome journey across the plains. Doubtless nearly all of them, in the vernacular of the Western mountains, have "crossed over the range."

A NOTE ABOUT THE PRINTING

This first regular edition is limited to 650 copies, designed and printed by Jack D. Rittenhouse at his Stagecoach Press in Santa Fé. Body text was set in Linotype Caledonia, with chapter headings handset in old French Ionic. Printed on a hand operated press, using Hamilton Kilmory paper. A special "Wagonmaster Edition" was also printed, limited to 99 copies. No further printings are planned by the Press.